Odalisque

in

PIECES

Camino del Sol

A Latina and Latino Literary Series

Odalisque

in

PIECES

Carmen Giménez Smith

THE UNIVERSITY OF ARIZONA PRESS

TUCSON

The University of Arizona Press
© 2009 Carmen Giménez Smith
All rights reserved

www.uapress.arizona.edu

Library of Congress Cataloging-in-Publication Data
appear on the last printed page of this book.

Publication of this book is made possible in part by the proceeds of a permanent
endowment created with the assistance of a Challenge Grant from the National
Endowment for the Humanities, a federal agency.

Manufactured in the United States of America on acid-free, archival-quality paper
containing a minimum of 30% post-consumer waste and processed chlorine free.

14 13 12 11 10   6 5 4 3 2

TO EVAN

Contents

III

IV

I

Photo of a Girl on a Beach

Once when I was harmless
and didn't know any better,

a mirror to the front of me
and an ocean behind,

I lay wedged in the middle of daylight,
paper-doll thin, dreaming,

then I vanished. I gave the day a fingerprint,
then forgot.

I sat naked on a towel
on a hot June Monday.

The sun etched the inside of my eyelids,
while a boy dozed at my side.

The smell of all oceans was around us—
steamy salt, shell, and sweat,

but I reached for the distant one.
A tide rose while I slept,

and soon I was alone. Try being
a figure in memory. It's hollow there.

For truth's sake, I'll say she was on a beach
and her eyes were closed.

She was bare in the sand, long,
and the hour took her bit by bit.

So You Know Who We Are

The wisteria and bill collectors colluded
to swallow our household whole, so we dismantled
it, rivet and splinter, made two piles on the lawn:

1. belongings the quality of lead,
2. belongings the quality of dandruff.

The blue stoop, its yellow roses,
a peep show each time we cracked the door,
my dog-eared book on serial killers,
the painting with the wandering eye—
stacked in the yard
as we had done a dozen times before.

My father insisted that staying
was akin to calcifying. He hated geologic
permanence buried in heaps under us.
He buried his employ instead.
My mother sewed nickels into her hem.

We children were assigned the task
of packing only the most relevant bits
into milk crates stolen from the grocery store.
The leave-behinds
we picked over:

a giant jar of buttons,

a red satin jumpsuit,

a doll with galaxies painted onto her eyes,

strands and strands of hair.

We wrote our names in tiny letters

on the walls of our rooms

to put down a trace of our stay.

Moonrock

My father stood watch

over night's deficient tide pool:

the weight of it so upon him,

he locked himself in the car to think.

By day he'd wear us

into onionskin. At night he'd flee

to the driveway, where he lived

in unkempt hair.

He was the phantom weeping

powdery tears into the ashtray.

He tattooed legal pads with a furious

manuscript about the world's

petty campaign to own him.

But then, I only saw the man

through glass, a disputed

and conspiratorial thing.

How It's Told

It was night and the light,

vague. My father, drunk.

The car creaked through the Bronx

because it had to. My brother's

sleep hum kept me awake.

I saw my father stop,

empty his gut

next to the open door.

The night with the shard moon,

my drunken father hummed

to keep awake. The wedding ring clinked

the steering wheel, the door yawned,

and the din of his retching, the stink of it.

The night and our frost-white

car lurched through the city.

My father, drunk on rum,

crackled like a live wire,

then went limp with sick.

We stopped where he could

give it up, then slunk off,

leaving it behind.

With each telling,

the city and we become more wasteland.

A small hill of broken dolls

in a lot, the battering

red lights, an iron-barred window.

A momentum broken in two, three, more . . .

The beer bottles in the cooler clinked,

and it was like watching the film of me,

the music scoring what I suspected.

A song, over and over,

tu me 'cistes brujera.

The engine's fan whirred

when the car stopped—

We left because the party ended.

When the tunnel called.

While the city watched, or didn't.

The door closed. The city left behind.

What we did because we had to.

The screen split in two, one side

light, the other dark.

Our Voices Occupy Rooms

We were a family of women, big on art. Not the kind gotten from travel,

thick-papered books, or the didactic analysis of a period in a classroom,

but rather the kind garnered from gaping at a painting, goose-skinned with awe.

Well into my years, I feel it in my body, activated samely

by the women in my family doing their cumbia, and when the goose bumps came

in the museums, my mother urging us to get right up in the painting's faces, I'd

remark loudly on the French parliaments, the rosy cheeks,

although my mother was most likely standing near the Dutch milkmaids.

And she would call back, *Yes! Wow!* We joke about volume in our family:

my sister's husky, raucous laugh, my aunt's melodic squeal, my mother's

operatic sneeze. All freight-train loud. I take large gulps of air

to fuel my oration. I worry terminally that people notice knowing that people

notice and so hoping that people realize there is little I can do to change it.

My friend Aida, beautiful in a '40s Varga way, has a voice that booms

like smoky electricity, an eel. She's brown too, but that suggests: look

at those people with their ways, their food, like when people assume

I like spicy food. I don't. Yet some native attributes are deep wells

of pleasure. In museums, my mother would call out to me over the gallery's

benumbed solemnity in her familiar and animal call: *¡Lizi, mira ésto!*

which, like a scent, gave me a chance to tingle in this most public place.

I have a place in my heart

for the girl who plays dangerous with powder.
She can skinny straight out of the fold
of caution and onto the lap of glory sweet, glory be!
and for her I sing.

She has even intentions and cartoon skin.
She handles snakes. She wraps bonbons. She fits the slot,

besides being a clairvoyant with great shoes.
How else was she to know about absolutes?
She walks past the boutiques. She won't take zero.
Once she found a cupboard
to crawl into and stayed
until the millennium floated far enough away.
That's the last story.
Here I bend her like a reed and whistle.

Dawn, Versified

We took pills and ideals. The backlit hills were blue against the sky, and the creamy
soignée element flared around us. Under dutiful watch, the almighty christ kind.

Torrential downplay of giggling. *I am sad to see you go.* Then the humpbacked lady with her,
such trying, walked past. We walked, too, but not the limping kind.

Limbed as fish or tree. Wired for longitude. We were just loving the grand earlyness
of walk. Some do: our kind.

Once I was walking with Dawn. The drills gone for Sunday. My duress was valentiney, not the deliverable kind.

Coincidence, then, with such a bomb shudder. The better part of it in the neck and gut.
The ground was as still as always, but the shift made us look, for heaven kind

came to earth to dimple our reverie. For that peculiar nod knowing where we were.
For that when two girls crossed came one, old and not kind.

Such fatuous noise we were, but necessary. Killing
time with cigarettes. Filling in the blade okay. Then was it.

Tree Tree Tree

There's that game we play:
Repeating a word until it ceases to mean

and it holds itself upon its sound

as if leaves and leaves and green and trunk
were not the end of this tree.

Meanwhile there is the ring in our ears, and

tree and tree have become a forest.
Trees give nothing, not even a sound.

Our tongues make branches move.

I Don't Want to Be a Ballerina Anymore

To bring in cash, I built a stage for the way my legs twinkled in the fenced-off garden that housed our old tricycle. I knew the pas de chat, the pas de deux, third position, and others I couldn't name but could do.

I never needed mirrors—neighbors climbed their roofs and took photographs with their mouths. I became a loose thing. I gave them shimmy, my body split into Trinidad: blue, rose, and amber.

The coins they threw were from all over. Some were useless. Some let me buy passage for my brother and me to the dark, cool theater where Bonnie and Clyde were laid flat with bullets. We'll go that way, I thought. I slipped coins into my mother's tip jar. What a precious little sacrifice I thought I was.

Still, I knew no one deserves a chance at everything, and I would have burned off my body like a wart if it meant the death of this particular irony: my family didn't make a peep. That's why, one week later, I sashed bags of lead to my ankles.

What She Meant

The early orange sun filtered into the room, but I feigned sleep,

lay still inside my smooth brown hands, eyes clamped shut.

The click of their tongues took inventory

of my failures, kept me awake,

and it would be morning soon. Plus I was engrossed.

I had failed, oh

had I. Ever.

They sparred over how I was

cursed with a susceptibility for one-way tickets.

Too emotional.

Had I ever heard of two weeks' notice?

What was wrong with telling the truth some of the time?

And what about the growing string of unpaid karmic debts?

Fooey! said the one on the left.

She should root down, stop starting over!

She should stop hiding beneath herself.

She should know by now there's such a gnarl in her—

The right one: grizzled and pissed.

Trouble and confusion breed light.

Don't like her much myself, but she's got better-than-nothing chances.

Her hands wove Medusa curls of prospect.

She tossed back the haze that was her cape,

and I floated through it like a daughter.

As I escaped out the kitchen window, I turned

for one last glance, and that's when they disappeared. This was new.

Finding the Lark

One.

Our house of Quiet Restraint
had so few gifts in it. My mother
lived quiet as a ring in a velvet box.

I wrote a poem about my father
turning into a planet, of being
that planet's anxious satellite,
rising from its orbit
into the atmosphere.
In the poems, I burned down
our modest house.
I burned down houses
all over town.

No one knew me, I thought.
But my mother did.
She scribbled me a picture
where my mouth should have been.
She explained longing
and offered me salves, furs,
cigarettes wrapped in linden leaves.

Two.

Every morning a lark

came to the front window

that framed her.

Arson is Invention, sang the lark

from her perch,

pointing to where her silvery heart smoldered.

I grew my mouth,

kissing that window,

roiling waters inside,

my hunger stretching

its feline limbs.

I wondered what her gifts were.

Wondered if the lark was my mother or

if my mother, my mother? Then one morning

the lark disappeared.

From my window I watched

for the desperate speck.

Searched the bushes. Searched the table,

her perch in the house's

veiled attic. The halo of smoke

in the sky was dotted with birds.

But they weren't the lark.

I watched the sky, pushed out of the window

to look, my long hair twisted in the wires

that connected our house

to the distance. A fire chattered.

I looked into the lacy face of it.

I didn't know where it came from.

I wanted it.

At first it seemed to me

that it was the truth

burning away.

Then, not at all.

Three.

I slept while my mother

measured my hunger.

She left cottage cheese in cardboard boxes.

She left a note on the door:

Gone. Don't Wait Up.

She found the photo

I took of the lark.

I adorned it with pearls. In it the lark sings

a song I tried to learn

from the cleft of her mouth.

I once pressed the photo to my face

like a mask, but nothing.

This my mother took.

Sweet. Sweet Girl. Sweet Girl of Mine.

She knew what I wanted all along.

Four.

My pencil grows sharper.

The ink runs full.

The cold wind stays at my back.

My father becomes a ghost of industry.

My mother wraps herself in cloaks

at night. Every night, she looks in the trees.

Su-weet, she calls out, searching for the source of smoke.

Sweet Girl. She becomes a stranger with sticks in her hair.

Lark, come home. Lark, find my mother. Now she's the one

who needs you. When my mother kisses me,

she tastes like soot.

Girl Moth

Handmaid Moth

In the corridor outside my bedroom:
a commotion about beauty.

The buzz—it burrows.

Someone has left the door open
to a white moth.

But she is so still.
Take a water glass from the kitchen and
trap her in that clarity.

Gypsy Moth

A moth is a tight swallow.

A moth is a deep, jealous spot on my grandmother.

I would fill a birdcage with moths,

dispatch it into an ocean where they could fly with fish.

Moths are often still.

Give me a moth and a shred of black silk,

and I'll show you history.

Luna Moth

Screen door, mothball, citronella,

poison, acrimony, newspaper.

Windowpane, formaldehyde, vaccination,

flytrap, silk tent, pesticide.

Frog, vanity, automobile,

flattened palm, pinch, and water.

I was death to begin with.

Io Moth

On the falsetto of a high wind,

a chorus of saints narrates landings. My children

collect armfuls of anise for my arrival,

and a clock ticks off the minutes.

A lake coughs up the god and goddess,

hammered from gold. They

crack a girl's skull to see inside.

From my perch in the sky I direct carvers

to scratch the earth with what I say before I shrink,

and I shrink, and I shrink.

Offer

To look numb upon a narrator writing her pink barest,

to eggshell a born bird, to throw up walls

and narrow her opening to one.

She will refrain

like a mirror. It's the sorcery in her tin box.

To quiet her, to fold the fragile lace of her face.

She sing so wrong—swift and noisy.

She flies from the cage to find herself quiet again.

Pillow Talk

I am an odalisque in pieces.
Frisson should happen every single time,

but doesn't. Instead it stammers
like a bike light.

You promise postcards
from the Atlantic Mirror,

then leave scarabs under
your thumbprint.

My gypsy window:
your fissure.

Listen, I got here
the same way you did,

taking heart in a stranger
who plucked music from my pudendum,

so make something true
before you go. Or don't.

I'll find it.
My kind always does.

Cities, I Still Love You

Where did the picture come from, someone says,

feeling the signature of wings in her chest.

The monument: We cleaned ourselves in its genesis,

and left it up because, come on, like it wasn't hollow,

a spectacle not meant for the museums we start like families.

O this pittsburgh, its hallucination of throwing a drink

into the west's face. That's where I kept us.

We got cornered, and our pockets were turned out.

Our hours were borrowed, a delirium no one could name

fled into us. Now we pay and pay.

Every face is someone else we know and as true as the exile

we woke into once, before we even had a chance to visit.

How to Splint Things on the Run

Take the nearest escape route and find yourself the fig tree. Find its best arm, buried in the topmost canopy, and snap it loose with your one good hand. Press it against that one day from History until you make friction. This might require a binding. Compress until it all goes white and you can't see what went upended. Cinch the edges of the wound until it spells out your name, murmurs it like the lover did. Wrap your own body over the wound so it becomes center hollow. Do this for forty minutes, and in the meanwhile retrace your steps to curse yourself. It happens, but never to you. Or it only happens to you, at times like this, to the one you love, etc.

Wrap it with silk, if it's handy, or wrap it with the best scarf you own. It should be a token fraught with scents. Hold your arm/leg/elbow over healing fire (the one that's left burning all day) for minutes you count with your heartbeat. Repeat until layer after layer singes away. There will be little left but the glowing bone. That's what you've wanted: to get back at it, to see it still humming with poignancy.

Pluck out a thimbleful of marrow and drink it. That's your final step. That and all the limping home you'll do, buzz like a desk lamp for 15 to 30. What's left hairline will get fickle in the rain.

Casanova Variation

He unfolded his mouth around mine in the moon's puddle. The astronomer in him charted the moles on my face. Hours wet-strinded our pillow. His, the face with twenty sides. One widow, peaked and pale. Another, feathery.

"We will travel downward," he promised. "The love guarantee will arrive soon." And all because he had a list. When we were in, the instance froze for a hundred years.

There were no lines, only mumbled indecency of the sweetest kind. He spoke words bigger than my fist. I left, but my body was still ground in because that's what he most wanted.

I wound round him like a small town.

Casanova Variation

Today's death was *fantastic*.

Five hours pass
like a door opened just right, and afterwards,

my body made minuscule
because you asked.

It wound round like a small town
with persimmon-colored fields,

gullies round them,
the useless ligature of tongues, useless.

Still darkened, we
take your mouth ideas around back.

Casanova Variation

If he were new, I would wear a dress

I've never worn. His breath reeks.

Addresses are hard to find.

The name, the number.   *Gasp.*

Night, a membrane. Stars shoot into us.

A blue jay visits my bird feeder.

I would try again, if he were a dress I'd never worn.

The Ever

I grew it under the house
where the loamy spores live.

I jilted my friends for it.
I sandbagged around it
when the first flood came.

When the second one came,
I held it up over the swirling water
until my shoulders hurt
and I had to hand it over.

So it would look authentic,
I burned the edges of it.

I put it in someone else's mouth.

It deposited a droplet
of itself into me so that
I became that thing,
that nameless, shameless
thing wound around
a limb on an apple tree.

I whispered in its ears
the fraught lyrics
of my girlhood, *please,*
please tell me now,
like I could have anything from it.

I lived on it.
It followed me in the subway
and provoked
me to buy skirts that cinched
me vapid.

It was chronic
like an earache:
the vertigo, the slowing,
and the brackish taste of the cure.

It was mine,
so I hid it from you.

It crumbled
like marzipan.

I hid it deep in the velvet
nose of the animal that sleeps
at the foot of the bed.
It was so far in the black
that when you looked,
I pretended to help.

The animal lay still,
and you set your hands
on her to look for it.

But I found it, and it impressed
itself on the pad of my thumb,
a burn to fret over.

It gathered our beds,

their frost, this last bend in our eon.

Gathered into its chest

feathers and the idea of feathers,

flight and urge,

the thing all along.

An Archipelago

~

A tremulous bell chills the lighthouse. The sea reveals a hem
to the wife, her hand in a bucket that swallows.
Anchored to the horizon, the harbor scrawls in a boat's face.
The morning is backdrop to wives waving their men away.

~

The fishermen leave for the heave-ho of spirit.
A narrow sunbeam holds them hostage to the water.
It's their way in, but also the sun's
indifference, the violet pause of it.

~

The men cast their nets around the edge and catch mercury fish,
still them with their hands to give to their wives, the ones made
famous for their voices. This island is about fury. If you erase
the plot and the setting, you'd see the icon's
customary influence, enormous and acquisitive.

~

The tides create strain between the ocean and the wives.
The islands float, secular and coy, as if in the ocean's palm. The wives
gather to pray: *Safe Harbor: Each hour's yawn.*
Make my body always element.
Feather or agate with a vein through it, or the deep,
stasis. Make me a force of ruin: books, photos, letters.
To soak into rugs and make a stench of them.

Trains That Hurtle

The boy wearing headphones and leaning

against the brick wall is the visual perch

I cling to until the train comes.

According to my horoscope, he'll rescue me

from scrutiny. Gravity's stitched me good into Earth's skirt,

and I don't know if I'll ever get into the galaxy.

In the year of Questions, No Answers,

I get the raver kid from Bakersfield

to muzzle me from crying, drunk dialing,

and falling in love with despots.

Thank God for public transportation

and all its resistant bodies. For this random collusion,

which makes everything

bright and sharp. I'm reinvented here.

A second chance and the train comes on time

to give the whole thing ballast. The kid shoots me a smile

like I'm some stranger, like we don't have history.

Maybe it really is Mercury in retrograde,

like my astrologer said. The planet floating backwards,

whirling some of us older than the stars, some of us nascent and bare.

Fortune: A Conversation

Your dream in which the ceiling dilated over us
was a vision, and
the boats you had also seen—spectacles near in time—

were still looming.
What you have to know is buried,
pushed away like a bone that unearths

only when a dog is ready for it.
What you hide jewels you,
that acute examination.

Your twin lives only to explain
you're against his false backdrop.
When you pause there to look in on you,

a discovery is made.
Your facsimile retains
your misunderstandings, but
with nothing of the original spirit. Illuminating.

Take this hindsight like a wallet
of cash, exchange it for the local currency, you
endless inversion. You optimist.

Eyelash

I wish the preoccupation with diamonds wasn't such a hinge
or that I lived like a starlet's eyeball.
I wish I could spout blasphemy quick as motorcycles.
I wish for my bloody caul back.

Wanted: A big, fat organism to eat me alive.

I wish that everyone in my stomach would stop scratching.
I would like to be raised over the crowd in a palanquin,
pretty please.

Will someone write me a proper response?

I dream Manhattan gets cheaper.
That these things are cheaper:
Drugs, daintiness, the little mock dress.

I wish for a bit back, five or ten cents' worth,
a favor, a door, a crumb from the one that got away.

I wish I could find what I need like you find a twenty
in an old coat. I wish I could unravel it all and start
it again with new wool flecked silver. To redo each first day.

I want to choose right. I want the look
and the feel of authenticity. I'm thirsty, hungry,
peaked in lust. A cavern of aching yen.
I want, I want, I want. It's got a ring to it. I want the ring.

Solve for N

So I chased myself into whirlwinds, then
drifted past the audience of wheat
like a waft of unspecified rot waiting to be diffused.

A field of husbands dithered and stammered
outside of my head. One of them lived hours
away from me. He hid his indoors deeper in.
Then it became just like dying. The sun
burned me into a new air to drift more,
my questions got left. I fixed myself to weather vanes
when I wanted an address and unfurled like a dollar bill
when it was time. I was a bad dance caught
in a record scratch waiting to be cut into.

I faded out when that didn't happen.
I got out of it by curtsying until I was raw-knuckled from dragging.
I became my own tax and saw paths spin into a web
of fragments without subjects.

Translation

I left you sleeping in a city like this—you were better off without me.

I'm cinder and you're wind, which justifies my absence.

The gestures you turned into castles were only nothing at all.

A fortress always dissembles.

Oh yes, the imprint of your finger doesn't make you godlike.

But the jar in every woman's heart makes her a nun.

You talked like there was an Italy we'd go to together.

When I was elegant and pearl-like, nobody loved me.

Looking

Right before she disassembled:

outside of the room

the gilt mirror hanging in the hallway

captured a chip—a forehead,

an eyebrow—resurrected the face,

a ghost she had once feared,

then outgrown.

Ghost of no backward glance.

Of map-face, lined with momentum and excess. An other

mirror. She had been sure until then

that the conjured stranger was all

she would leave.

Why I Left

When the sun tilted face down into the chunky redwood
tree line and the chill air was stereo time,
you know, getting it going because
the nights were long and cool affairs,
I called it affection, not love,
and was comforted thusly. For knowing the difference.

But one night I awoke with a pain
that divided me. I whimpered quietly and with shame.
To need and to want in such loneliness. But he heard and
held my belly in his hands like a sorcerer would.

Still, time passed and I began to mislay
the books I had set aside to read later.
The air smelled like expectation, which distracted.
Keys disappeared. Purse lost.
Over dinner I asked if he had seen my hairbrush.
Without an answer, he brushed the ghost from my face.

Elegy for the Gone Husband

How is it we announced our names

with such scuffed marbles in our mouth,

sheathed ourselves in that felt-lined bed,

crafted dream props, undid vexation with spit and come?

How did the rolling swarm always swerve

past our house on the shifting hill?

When did alteration spring these impostors upon us—

my delirium, my frayed sleeve, the end to my clauses?

Geothermic Properties of Fire

What happens when breath stills:
snow—
the swallow, the swindle.

She returns to the core: combustible, blue, veined with glyphs.

Gravity has etched her. She's the oldest cartographer,
the plotter of maps into feudal squares.

She says it's graphic in nature, but don't believe her.
Age leaves her with vanity, but not
with the way a body saves itself.

Give her air and she reaches
deeper—peels back a stone
and finds water,
takes like a magnet takes.

Wherever he's gone isn't far enough.
Reckless, her nails catch on trees.

Red Litany

She was angry that it rained
that the thunder made gossip

that the steam on the window knew
that no one was

that there was a mirror
that the mirror closed her eyes

that amnesia felt floating
that she knew

that really there was nothing
that she was falling

that the gift was a fraud
that the party was useless

that the message was sent
that she had given her hand

that she had turned into red
that someone wore her

that the walking stopped
that the singing stopped

that a bird ignored her

that the neighbors had it

that there was daytime

that nighttime was no better

that it didn't fit

that it did.

Lapsarian

There's the original, then there's the copy.

To resist the arrangement,
his nights became her days,
and she lit upon his desire with papery wings
because she could. Because the droning voice
sounded like the hemming and hawing
cicadas in the grass.

Every morning he keened
and she denied. Every night she crept
into his sleep and spilt him like milk.

So easy to snap him awake
under the moon's impassive face.
By day she slept in the hollow of a tree
while the sun set hot shimmer upon them.

He wanted, and so did this place. It wanted
with the stiff sounds the voice made of it.
The voice had more to name,
more to instruct. *This one is for eating.*
Put it over the fire.

Half her, half voice, a pale boy, all need,
his hand on her shoulder,
the voice saying things like, *river runs over rocks.*

Frogs and flies, on the edge of water mostly.

He was come from her.

The voice misunderstood.

She had been the heft

that the wind bore down to two.

To not be form and then be it.

That had been her first crash.

Little populated, that landscape.

She had wanted to put her own mouth

to work, but the voice kept interrupting.

Around them, tree after tree,

soft bending grass,

and two, three flowers.

A lion chewing lazily on a lamb's leg.

Nothing else but the voice

droning in lead-heavy detail:

The sky turns blue, then black flecked with white.

What comes first?

The thing behind the voice,

or the idea fitting the voice around it?

At first the voice went out at night—

things weren't all made yet.

At night she heard the whip

of a thing coming up, then nothing for a while

until another thing.

She wanted her own sounds

for the shapes her eyes discerned

while he slept like a thumb,

the unblinking owl her companion.

Owl—the sounds of its eyes.

Blink—black, then blacker, a night twitch.

Ache—what's gray and hollow.

Coleoptera, yes. The black shell, said the voice.

Sometimes she hollowed out a sound like trembling

when the clamor of the world being born

became too much, a song to reside in, the sound of

the whole world opening up its mouth

since the world was young, and

now the sound was rising in her: *Escape.*

Become the uneasy long thing with no name.

But where she looked for a road,

there was none.

She looked up and saw only

the sky's flaccid glow, first blue, then gray, then black.

She looked at him too in the dangerous light.

So she began naming the vast maw

beyond the voice's borders,

which contains

several mouths,

a helix reaching deep into the center,

the hammock of her bones, made to live in.

The voice talked over her. It elided her

with description. And when she didn't budge,

the sky's face grew sodden,

tore open to smother her,

because when a home fails,

legacy is involved: Trees stop growing

when someone refuses to give up the earth.

This is the part between parts.

The pause between the verses.

IV

Vacation As Prelude

The amniotic Pacific, years ago,
brittle and gray as I gulped it
when a wave took me under.

My fingers became,
through the sun flash and water,
the ebony of burnt twig.

I tumbled for eternities
without air, no body
either, just the core,
then got spit out
onto the shore, *and this
is almost dying*,
I said to myself. Chance reminded
me my claws were tenuous.
The flesh of tourists and children
were ember pillars
in my stung, burnt retinas.

In drowning,
literal, metaphorical,
a friend said today,
one lets go of will
or becomes the shrapnel of it.

She, As a Veil

I gave a lecture in the Hall of Months: The Truth in the
Echo. One where words, above ribbons of song,

touched the Other, then ruptured—like a question,
shine and curve with over-divided sound.

I spoke of the exploded view, the precise diagram:
form disregarding function, the me showing,

and I told of elements I did not know myself—
truth making its end appearance.

Or the woman, that tree marked for a
silence. Secrets lasting. The vision

we put deep into ourselves, in on the closing door of
Eternity as moment, this naming yesterday

that we need when least expected, making our
gesture. A door closed the past-again way.

Clumsy

The scars I have—the plot of traveling
with too little eye. Reaching through
mulberry for a lost ring, I've bloodied my arms
like saints do. My bones and I:
swindled by gaps in the sidewalk.

I live like the earth's moving faster
than we are. I split my head following the wrong
trajectory. The world marks me with its vagaries.
Or it's me pushing against the day's thick flannel,
a vertigo straining against its seams.

Déjà Vu

It happened to me once.

Winter came, and snow quilted every inch.

I stood on the soapbox, as I was told,

and made staggering accusations. The public ignored,

so I retreated behind the potted yew.

I was waiting for a moment I was supposed to have

on a balcony overlooking the giant, gridded landscape.

The sounds I made underscored what I meant.

The potted yew was the face that I wore.

It was a metaphor for what could be.

The public endured.

I put the potted yew behind me. I made staggering an art.

That wasn't the truth though. Winter

comes and negates all it covers. It doesn't matter where I stand.

The balcony is a floor without walls.

The yew is a hurt that shadows.

The instance lives beneath us. Not just us, everybody.

The shadow hurts us. I make sounds like

the truth. Fate and theft are involved.

I think I told you this before. The floor is a wall that obscures.

The yew is a quilt without color. Shadow is a fate you involved.

The yew on a balcony negates. I told you this before.

I was left undone. It's what I meant. Underneath everyone.

Heart Display

Wake up. The whole place is waking up.

Morning is a division of black from water debt.

Look into the eyes of your favorite face.

The irises are taut with sermons

about affliction, and still, some nights don't ever fully end.

A dream about decline deepens the dark

with ugly reason. A sedative approaches,

and you wait not to hear.

You're boiling water inside the desolate kitchen.

You're playing music for a never-broken tonight.

A word-riddled hum and green tea and

steam fill your mouth. You

stand in a bowl of fluorescence

because it begins through a film of fog.

Blue swims around you until you come to your senses,

but life is a peacock. You are not.

At the center of the kitchen light: each mark,

each line makes you grave.

Daughter

You're a trace that won't vanish,
the snow that falls off silence,
the wordless gap. You're the clue found
in the corner. The body as simple dust.

You're the spider thrill of spring,
the season that swings its mood
into our room, my in-light buzz.

Your small, thin body, the late-burning
lamp, the walls and their spells.
You leave humidity on our pillow,
a corona. You're the return to only.

Prepartum

So long I resisted biology, ashamed of its elephantine

and industrial geographies.

Now, swept clean of gamine,

I read pabulum with diagrams of my progress.

In this reductive state,

none of the gilt edge I fancy. If I were

the ocean, I'd be the ocean

receding then cresting at the moon's whim.

My son, embedded in me like a black pearl,

calls up awe and, in the vise grip

of our contract, secret woe.

I bubble with benign fatalism,

leak as a cell does.

The Drive Home

My son is my newest nerve—

too small to speak, mouthpiece for death.

Why I never leave the house.

When he gets ensnared inside the treads

of his crying, I'm seized:

the other naïf in the car,

the one with the barest idea

of what costume to wear. *Mother? Really?*

My outside holds my inside together

with the flimsy bandage of duty. I think, *Stop,*

so I pull into a parking lot

to wait it out. His eyes howl glass shards

into my head while I struggle to undo the space-traveler

clasps that keep him bound inside the car,

but facing away from me so that he only sees

what we leave behind, like he's forgiving as he goes along.

Sightings

In case the subject comes up: I've left behind
a crazy mask, a moment with a windowpane.
I love the multifaceted when there are only two or three.

You are my inverse. It's eternity to get inside,
but that's okay: I'll wait up to fifty times (I've counted).

In the Buenos Aires airport, I saw you sitting with three
bird-like women who had long hair.

At a hotel in Montmartre, I heard your sigh
let loose. Then the music went loud, so it was all I could do.

Climbing down the stairs stealthily, so many dictions to find.

Could I suggest a better architecture than that?
All those arcs of air making your face.

All my life—trying to put something into it.
Intention doubles (at least) when anyone waits.

Idea in a Ruinous State

Only the flutter of an idea.
Only an absolute that throws off the cloak of mooniness
to reveal that she never was or never will be.
Only a promise to prevail over speech's vault.
After all day behind the broad face of memorandum,
only the shadow figure in the den. Only a giant fit snug in a matchbox.

Only chancellorette to the skyline twisted around heaven.
Only the fugue macaques hum from the orange trees.
Carmen, they call out from across the sea.
Only the vision that surrounds her
with a harmony that tastes of honey, or more so.

Only her house, a blur that shifts
as the earth shifts and is made true only here.
Only the invisible post where she writes the encounters
with air's lusters. Only the imagined hour
with which she's made a fragile craft.

Acknowledgments

26: "Sightings"

American Letters and Commentary: "She, As a Veil," and "Dawn, Versified"

Borderlands Poetry Review: "I have a place in my heart"

Boston Review: "Pillow Talk"

Brooklyn Rail: "Elegy for the Gone Husband," "Fortune: A Conversation"

Coconut Poetry: "Heart Display"

diode: "So You Know Who We Are"

Fairy Tale Review: "Finding the Lark"

Fourteen Hills Review: "Geothermic Properties of Fire"

Mandorla: "The Ever"

Minnesota Review: "Moonrock"

nocturnes: "Girl Moth"

Ocho: "I Don't Want to Be a Ballerina Anymore"

Ploughshares: "Déjà Vu"

Poetry: "Tree Tree Tree"

POOL: A Journal of Poetry: "Prepartum," "Solve for *N*"

Provincetown Arts: "Photo of a Girl on a Beach"

Shampoo Poetry: "Cities, I Still Love You"

Tusculum Review: "Idea in a Ruinous State"

The poem "How to Splint Things on the Run" is for Eric McKinley. The poem "Dawn, Versified" is dedicated to Dawn Murphy. The poem "Finding the Lark" is dedicated to Kari Bradley.

The author would also like to thank Mary Jo Bang, Sheila Black, Richard Greenfield, Brenda Hillman, Evan Lavender-Smith, Kevin McIlvoy, Connie Voisine, and Mark Wunderlich for their help with this manuscript.

About the Author

Carmen Giménez Smith is the author of *Casanova Variations* (Dos Press, 2010), *Glitch* (Dusie Kollectiv, 2009), and a memoir forthcoming from the University of Arizona Press. Her writing has recently appeared in *Poetry*, *American Letters & Commentary*, *Ploughshares*, *Boston Review*, *Chicago Review*, *Colorado Review*, *Ocho*, *Mandorla*, *sleepingfish*, and many other magazines and journals.

Formerly a Teaching-Writing Fellow at the Iowa Writer's Workshop, she is now an assistant professor of creative writing at New Mexico State University, the publisher of Noemi Press, and the editor-in-chief of *Puerto del Sol*. She lives in Las Cruces, New Mexico, with her husband and their two children.

Library of Congress Cataloging-in-Publication Data

Giménez Smith, Carmen, 1971–

  Odalisque in pieces / Carmen Giménez Smith.

    p. cm.—(Camino del sol)

  ISBN 978-0-8165-2788-5 (pbk. : alk. paper)

  I. Title.

PS3607.I45215O33   2009

811'.6–dc22   2008053314